BRAVER
Stronger
SMARTER

First published in the United States in 2020 by Sourcebooks

Published by Sourcebooks eXplore, an imprint of Sourcebooks Kids
P.O. Box 4410, Naperville, Illinois 60567–4410
(630) 961-3900
sourcebookskids.com

Originally published as *Turn Off, Live On* in 2018 in United Kingdom by Wren & Rook, an imprint of Hachette Children's Group, part of Hodder & Stoughton.

Source of Production: Versa Press, East Peoria, Illinois, USA
Date of Production: April 2020
Run Number: 5018513

Printed and bound in the United States of America.
VP 10 9 8 7 6 5 4 3 2 1

BRAVER
Stronger
& SMARTER

Vincent Vincent

sourcebooks
eXplore

For Noah and Kitty,
keep shining brightly!

CONTENTS

INTRODUCTION

Do you sometimes feel like you're rushing from one thing to the next? Answering messages and group chats, taking pictures to post online, and then dashing out to see a friend before binge-watching every episode of an amazing new show?

The hustle and bustle of online life can be overwhelming, making us feel anxious or sad, while sometimes stunting our creativity and damaging our memories. After all, who needs to remember stuff if you can grab your phone and check the internet for answers?

Look around you next time you're out and about, and chances are you'll see more than one person staring mindlessly at their smartphone or tablet, totally oblivious to the world around them.

But it's so easily done, isn't it? You check your phone for a message and suddenly realize you've spent ages looking at cute cat clips on Instagram and watching videos about making fluffy rainbow unicorn slime. I've done it more times than I can remember—and I still can't make fluffy rainbow unicorn slime!

I'm not saying phones and tablets are bad—they can be seriously fun and really useful—but they're made to make us want to use them as much as possible, which can lead to problems.

That's because our phones are designed to trigger the pleasure-related parts in our brain, which release a chemical called dopamine. Dopamine has many roles, but one of the most important things it does is make us feel good when we behave in a certain way. And these feelings make us want to keep doing whatever made us feel so happy! When this is applied to behavior like eating food, it's really helpful, as it makes us want to find our next delicious meal. But the same science can be applied to smartphones and tablets. We are always checking and playing with our devices because we are seeking a quick pleasure boost, but this also means that they easily become quite addictive.

When I discovered this, it made me wonder how much time I'd get back if I wasn't spending so long using my phone. So I decided to try an experiment. I deleted all the social media apps from my device, turned off my notifications, and started leaving it in other rooms when I was at home.

It wasn't long before I noticed I had a **LOT** more time for other things—like reading books, baking cakes, and getting creative. I didn't stop using my phone, but I did change the way I used it, and it felt way better than I'd imagined it would!

Smartphones, tablets, and computers are all here to stay, and that's great. But I wanted to write something that could help give you more control over when and where you use this technology, and hopefully remedy the negative effects it can have on you too.

With smart exercises, activities, puzzles, confidence boosters, and relaxation techniques, this book aims to help you unleash your creativity, build your confidence, find calm, and exercise your brain cells. So, when you next feel the urge to shadow your enemies, Instagram your dinner, or try out the new Snapchat filter, you can free yourself from your phone and pick up this book instead!

I hope you enjoy it.

VINCENT

Admit it, have you ever felt frustrated, irritated, or fed up about someone's overly positive and bigheaded posts online?

You know the ones—when someone implies their vacation is the best trip anyone has *ever* been on, acting like they've just tumbled out of bed, even though everything about their posed selfie looks completely *perfect*, or like they're busy having an *amazing* time at the best party ever thrown.

Well, if this kind of content has ever gotten under your skin, you're not on your own. Around 40 percent of the world's population uses social media now, and while it's great for keeping us connected with our friends and what's happening around the world, spending too much time on apps like Snapchat and Instagram can actually have a pretty negative effect.

Our phones and tablets are amazing machines, offering us 24/7 access to comments, posts, and profiles. But while we use them, we are also bombarded by images of everyone else looking super-happy and successful, even when we might be feeling down in the dumps.

Deep down, we know that this isn't a real representation of someone's life and that they are posting a filtered version of their experiences. But we can still find ourselves comparing our lives and feeling like we don't measure up. And this can then trigger our anxiety, break our confidence, and leave us with unrealistic expectations of life and friendships. Like why aren't our vacations as fun? Why don't we look as good first thing in the morning? And why aren't we that popular?

Social media is here to stay, and the chances of people presenting their lives unfiltered are practically zero. But the good news is now that you've got this book, you're in a prime position to take control and improve your relationship with your online self.

Tackle the following tasks and you'll soon be kissing **FOMO** goodbye, paying less attention to phony posts, and feeling more confident about where you are and where you're heading.

Ready?

Let's go!

HELLO THERE!

First things first—let's introduce ourselves. My name's Vincent. I like finding happiness in random places, daydreaming about adventures, and doodling on whatever I can find.

What's your name? Write it in the box below.

Now, think about the following questions...

How does writing your name with a pen or pencil feel?

How is it different from typing it on a phone or tablet?

Grab a pen or pencil and draw a picture of yourself as you imagine **OTHER** people see you.

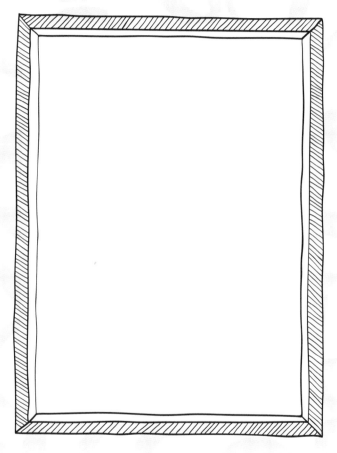

This time, draw a picture of yourself and think about how you **WISH** people saw you.

Now compare your pictures. What do they have in common? You! You can't control how other people see you. So the only thing that matters is how you see yourself—and you are amazing!

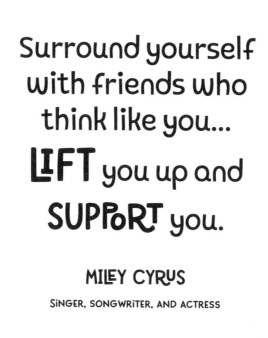

Surround yourself
with friends who
think like you...
LIFT you up and
SUPPORT you.

MILEY CYRUS

SINGER, SONGWRITER, AND ACTRESS

Social media sites are full of people giving the impression their lives are perfect, but this is just an illusion. No one's perfect and neither is anyone's life.

Your **IMPERFECTIONS** are what make you **SPECIAL.** Celebrate being different by listing them on this page!

☆ .... ☆

☆ .... ☆

☆ .... ☆

☆ .... ☆

☆ .... ☆

☆ .... ☆

☆ .... ☆

Now check off the statements that apply to you...

I am proud of my imperfections.

I'm learning to love being different.

I don't compare myself to anyone else.

Sometimes we can feel like we don't have much power, but problem-solving tasks can help, and they're fun too! Let's try something with the letters that make up **I AM STRONG.**

How many words of three letters or more can you find in the circle above? Each word must use the center letter plus two or more of the other letters. No letter can be used more than once in a single word.

Write the words you find on this page.

CAN YOU
FIND OVER
TWENTY
WORDS?

Circle the words in this panel that sum up how you felt when you finished this exercise.

PLEASED   SURPRISED

   BRAINY   Disappointed

Determined   RELIEVED

   DEFEATED   CLEVER

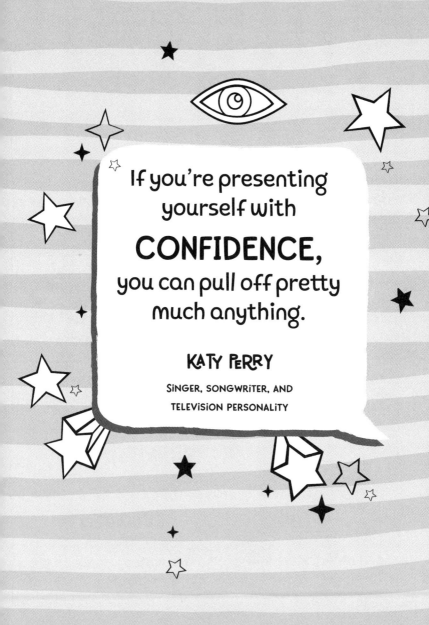

If you're presenting yourself with

CONFIDENCE,
you can pull off pretty much anything.

KATY PERRY

SINGER, SONGWRITER, AND TELEVISION PERSONALITY

Things are very simple on social media. Posts are either liked or ignored. But real life has a lot more detail, which gives us a much more accurate way of seeing things.

Try filling in the gaps of my story...

The girl combed her hair, put on her favorite _____ , and took a selfie. She then posted the photo online, got straight into her _____ , ate _____ , and watched _____ at _____ for the rest of the night.

Now turn the book upside down and read the story again; the missing words have been added...

The girl combed her hair, put on her favorite top, and took a selfie. She then posted the photo online, got straight into her pajamas, ate pizza, and watched Netflix at home for the rest of the night.

I bet you didn't fill in all the gaps correctly! That's because it's easy to misinterpret things when you don't have all the facts. Remember that people might post a filtered version of their lives online, but it's only half the story.

CIRCLE any of the phrases on this page that you've ever found yourself thinking.

THIS IS IMPOSSIBLE!

I'M AMAZING!

I'm so happy!

HOW MANY LIKES?!

I CAN'T BE THAT POPULAR.

I'M CLEVER.

I WISH THAT WERE ME.

I'M SO LUCKY!

I'll do better next time.

I'M SUCH AN IDIOT.

I'LL NEVER BE ABLE TO DO THIS.

YES! BRiLLiANT!

NOBODY LIKES ME.

I AM CONFIDENT.

Did you circle more positive or negative phrases?

Add more **THOUGHTS** that you find yourself thinking on this page.

Are these phrases more positive or negative?

Now, try speaking to yourself like you'd talk to your best friend. Be kind and remember: no one's perfect!

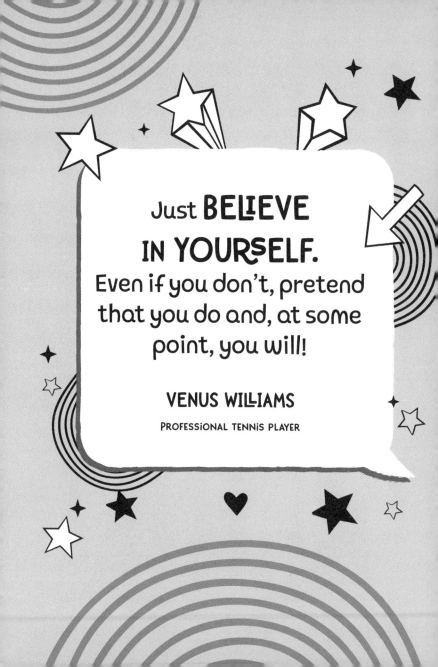

Just **BELIEVE IN YOURSELF.**
Even if you don't, pretend that you do and, at some point, you will!

VENUS WILLIAMS

PROFESSIONAL TENNIS PLAYER

Social media sites can knock our self-esteem, but your imagination can help. Make a **MIND-MOVIE** and tap into all that confidence you thought you never had!

Find somewhere quiet, get comfortable, and close your eyes.

Imagine you're sitting in a theater. What can you see from your seat when you picture the room? How does the seat feel?

Think about something you want to feel more confident about. Perhaps it's meeting new people, scoring an important goal, or passing a test.

Imagine the theater plays a movie about you. How do you look on the screen?

The film shows you being successful. You meet new people and get on brilliantly, your goal wins the match, or you get top marks in the test!

Make your movie as vivid as possible, adding lots of detail. Then add your emotions. How does the film make you feel? Are you calm and focused, or excited and happy, or something else?

Watch your mind-movie a few times, and you'll feel great. Repeat this exercise whenever you want to feel more self-assured!

THE MORE REALISTICALLY YOU ARE ABLE TO **VISUALIZE** A SUCCESSFUL OUTCOME, THE MORE **CONFIDENT** YOU WILL FEEL!

List four achievements that you're **PROUD** of and color the face that represents how nervous you were before each one.

.... 😟 😐 🙂

.... 😟 😐 🙂

.... 😟 😐 🙂

.... 😟 😐 🙂

It's natural to feel a bit nervous before a challenge, but did you worry for no reason? Bear this in mind and list your achievements again, rating how you would have felt if you had focused on a positive outcome.

.... 😟 😐 🙂

.... 😟 😐 🙂

.... 😟 😐 🙂

.... 😟 😐 🙂

Now list ten things you'd like to achieve in the future. Will you be as nervous about them? Come back and rate how you felt before each one after they're done.

.... ☹ 😐 🙂

.... ☹ 😐 🙂

.... ☹ 😐 🙂

.... ☹ 😐 🙂

.... ☹ 😐 🙂

.... ☹ 😐 🙂

.... ☹ 😐 🙂

.... ☹ 😐 🙂

.... ☹ 😐 🙂

.... ☹ 😐 🙂

Tricky situations aren't always as bad as we think and focusing on how things really are boosts our confidence!

When it comes to social media, there are just times I **TURN OFF** the world... Sometimes you have to give yourself space to be **QUIET**, which means you've got to set those phones down.

MICHELLE OBAMA

LAWYER, WRITER, AND
FORMER U.S. FIRST LADY

Social media has a knack for making you feel like you're missing out on cool stuff. A great way to beat **FOMO** is to remind yourself of good things in life that you might be taking for granted.

Fill this box with the stuff in your life that makes you happy.

Focusing on what you're grateful for will make you feel good, less stressed, and more confident too!

Now let's focus on **DOING** things that make you happy...

LIST THINGS YOU LOVE DOING	WHY YOU ENJOY DOING THEM

Look at this page whenever you feel like you're missing out, and remember: you're not competing with anyone!

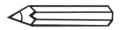

Instead of comparing yourself to other people online, focus on recognizing when things go well in real life.

Revisit this page and **COLOR** in a heart every time something good happens. Lots of positive stuff happens every day and this exercise will help you notice it more!

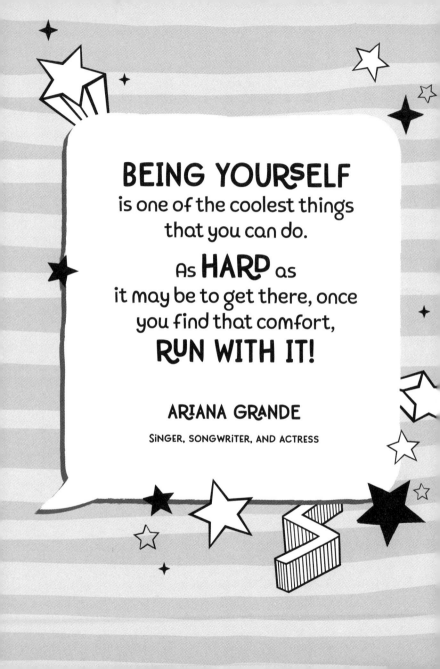

BEING YOURSELF
is one of the coolest things
that you can do.

As **HARD** as
it may be to get there, once
you find that comfort,
RUN WITH IT!

ARIANA GRANDE
SINGER, SONGWRITER, AND ACTRESS

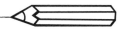

DOODLE things that you'd like to change about your life on this page.

What can you learn from each of these things?

. . . .

. . . .

. . . .

. . . .

Even stuff we don't enjoy can teach us about how we feel and help us become a happier person!

Fill these speech bubbles with **NICE** things people have said about you. Revisit this page whenever your mood needs lifting.

Now give someone else a compliment—you might just make their day!

Most people look down to use their smartphone or tablet, but research has shown this posture is bad for our necks and backs, and can have a negative effect on our mood.

Try these tips to avoid the **SMARTPHONE SLUMP**. They will have you feeling fantastic in no time!

1 Hold your phone at eye level when you're texting and avoid tilting your head. This will force you to hold your head, neck, and shoulders in a better position.

2 If you have to hold your phone lower, tilt your eyes to look at the screen, rather than your whole head.

3 If you're at home, lie down on your back with your knees bent and feet flat on the floor to use your phone. This will allow the muscles of your neck and upper back to relax.

4 Use voice dictation to text whenever you can so you're typing less!

If your neck feels sore, slowly move your head from side to side to stretch the muscles. Try gently moving your head back and looking up too.

CREATIVITY UNLEASHED!

So, now that we've dealt with social media, boosted our self-confidence, and discovered how we'd love to spend our time, it's time to tackle creativity.

Whether you realize it or not, creativity is a huge part of your life. Take a look around you. No matter where you are, chances are you'll see something that was created by someone. A lamppost? Someone designed it! A chocolate bar? Someone came up with the recipe! The chair you're sitting on? Someone invented that too!

But creativity doesn't just involve making things. For example, if you're faced with a choice, you think creatively to make your decision. And if you need to tackle a difficult situation, you use your creativity to figure out how to solve the problem. The power of your imagination knows no limits and you have the ability to create whatever you want. Plus, creativity makes life a little more fun and interesting!

A creative approach can help you see things differently and is a great way to tap into your individuality. After all, no one else can create things exactly the same as you, because they're not you!

Though technology has many positive uses, it can distract us from being creative and doing fun, inventive things with our time. Who knows? There could be someone out there being completely distracted by their phone, when they could be designing an amazing new chocolate lamppost-chair, or something else that's totally bonkers but totally brilliant too!

So, next time you've got a few spare minutes or find yourself feeling restless, avoid the temptation to pick up your phone, and try unleashing some of the creativity that's bubbling inside you instead. There are all sorts of ways you can do this, from singing and dancing to painting, drawing, and writing! And this chapter is the perfect place to kick-start those creative juices and get that amazing imagination of yours flared up.

Ready to get more creative?

Let's get going!

Connect these dots in any order and see if you can **CREATE** a picture. There are no rules when it comes to creativity—you can create whatever you want!

SURROUND YOURSELF with people who are the **KETCHUP** to your **FRENCH FRIES**—they make you a **BETTER VERSION** of yourself.

GRACE HELBIG

COMEDIAN, ACTRESS, AND YOUTUBE PERSONALITY

Look out the window or across the room and **DRAW** what you see.

NO ONE ELSE WILL DRAW THE **SAME** IMAGE AS YOU.

EVEN IF THEY **COPY** YOUR PICTURE, IT WILL STILL BE **DIFFERENT!**

HAIKU (say hi-koo) is a type of traditional Japanese poetry written in three lines. These poems are really **CLEVER** and EASY to write, as they use just a few words to create a picture in the reader's mind.

The first and last lines of a haiku have five syllables and the middle line has seven syllables.

A syllable is a part of a word that is pronounced as a unit. For instance, the word "haiku" has two syllables: hai-ku.

Here's an example:

SCATTER HAPPINESS
SEE IT FLOAT LIKE CONFETTI
AND MAKE THE WORLD SMILE

Now write your own haiku! You can use some of the words on the opposite page to get you started.

WINTER · Bloom · Garden · Spring · SHORE · WATER · ONLY · Autumn · JOURNEY · HAPPY · People · Yellow · THUNDER · Between · Night · Flower · Sunshine · Sunset · Listen · House · SAD · ALWAYS · Summer · RAIN · FUNNY · DAWN · Sleep · Before · Snow · EXCITING

43

I think that's when your **CREATIVITY** is developed, when you're young. I liked the world of the **IMAGINATION** because it was an easy place to go to.

DAVID WALLIAMS

ACTOR, COMEDIAN, AND AUTHOR

Stare at this page and let your mind **WANDER** for a few minutes. Then write about or draw whatever you found yourself thinking about on this page.

Think about these questions:
How did daydreaming feel?
What thoughts drifted into your head?
What did your daydream reveal?

Scribble lightly on this page. Then color in the different shapes in your scribble to create a

MESSY MASTERPIECE.

Which hand do you usually use to write with? Try **DRAWING** your favorite animal with the other hand and see what you come up with.

Drawing with your nondominant hand will help you focus and allow you to see shapes in new ways!

Everyone loves superheroes. They fight evil and have amazing powers and pretty awesome costumes too. If you could have one superpower, what would it be? Try **DESIGNING** your superhero outfit:

REMEMBER, YOUR **INDIVIDUALITY** IS YOUR REAL **SUPERPOWER**— EMBRACE IT!

Playing music and singing along can make you feel great. Make a **MASH-UP** of your favorite lyrics to create a fun new song. Firstly, write some words from a tune you love here:

Now use some of those words to make a new song:

Being inspired by something or someone you already love or admire is a great way to kick-start your creativity.

Fill this box with **DOODLES**! Here are a couple to get you started:

What do you think your doodles say about you?

When we doodle, our minds are balanced between awareness and daydreaming, which is why it's great for relaxing, creating new ideas, and concentrating!

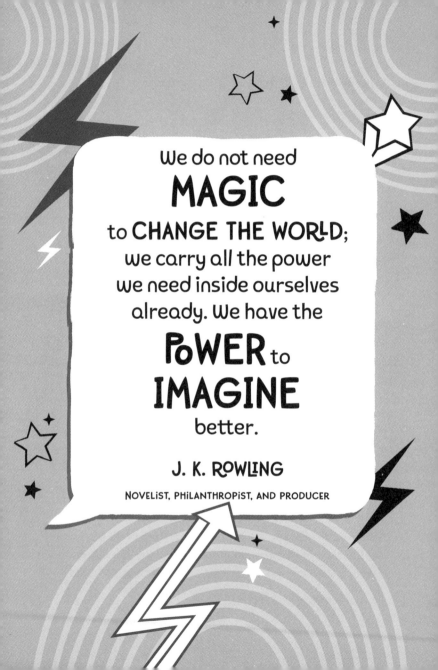

If you're finding it hard to be creative—for example, you might want to write a story but don't know how to start it—try **TAPPING** into your **MEMORIES**. Think about...

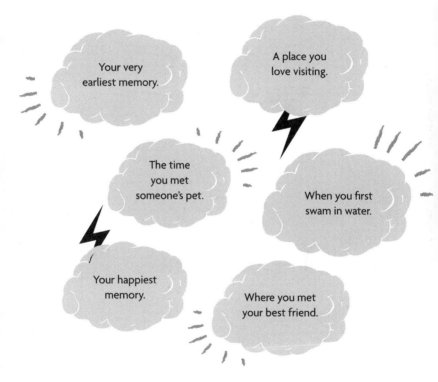

Your very earliest memory.

A place you love visiting.

The time you met someone's pet.

When you first swam in water.

Your happiest memory.

Where you met your best friend.

Now revisit your project and see if you have some new ideas. Thinking about the past will conjure up sights and sounds, places and people, that you can use as inspiration!

Fill this jar with **IDEAS**. Drawings, words, colors, stickers...
whatever you want! Just let it rip and get creating!

Now, get your thinking cap on! It's time for you to come up with **THE BEST APP EVER INVENTED**.

Think about these questions to get you started:

What would your app do? ....

How would it make people feel?

....

What would your app be called?

....

Draw your app in action!

Design your app's logo here.

Good work! Why not send your idea to an app developer? Maybe everyone will end up using your app one day!

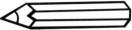

LIST five interesting words in this box.

DRAW three strange things in here.

DESCRIBE four moods in the box below.

Now begin a **STORY** involving the things listed on the previous page. Start writing, and don't stop until this page is full. Try not to think about your story—just write!

An amazing story can come from anywhere. This exercise helps you think outside the box!

Follow your **PASSION**, STAY **TRUE** TO **YOURSELF**, and never follow someone else's path. Unless you're in the woods and you're lost, and you see a path!

ELLEN DEGENERES

COMEDIAN, TELEVISION HOST, AND ACTRESS

Design a **COOL T-SHIRT** you think your best friend or a family member would like!

Transform these circles into recognizable **OBJECTS**, such as a button, soccer ball, or something else!

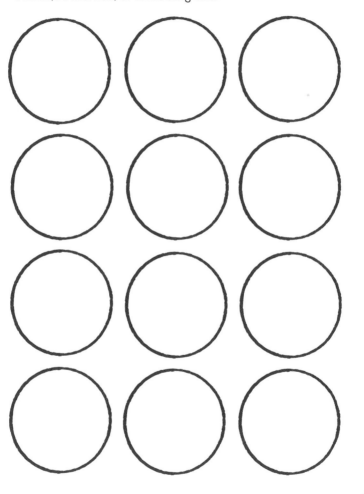

Creative inspiration can come from **ANYTHING**. Lay something, like a mug or a pencil case, on this page and draw around it. Then use the shape as the starting point for a picture.

Changing the way you look at things can give you a whole new perspective.

Here's a quick challenge: can you remember your best friend's phone number without checking your phone? Can you direct me to your local movie theater without checking the GPS? If you can't, you're definitely not on your own. We've become so reliant on our phones and computers to remind us about stuff, we often don't bother to remember things like phone numbers or directions.

That might not seem like a major issue, but our memory isn't just there to remember practical things like when we're going to the movies or if someone's birthday is around the corner. Our memory adds depth and color to our lives too, and remembering things we've done and challenges we've been through helps us learn from the past and grow.

Unfortunately, technology encourages us to do more than one thing at a time. For instance, you might pick up your phone to answer a message, and then suddenly realize you've spent forty-five minutes playing a game, texting friends, and taking selfies—all at the same time! It might seem fun, but it can mean we don't pay proper attention to what we're doing and easily get distracted.

Research has also shown that the part of our brain that is responsible for creating memories works best when we're actively engaged and focused on what's happening. But when we're on our phones, we're often not really fully concentrating and so, although we might spot something interesting as we quickly scroll through our feed, we often find ourselves not remembering what it was later on.

But don't worry, because your brain is one amazing piece of machinery that you can train to learn faster and remember more! And this chapter is here to help you do just that by boosting your brainpower and improving your memory with crafty riddles and mind-boggling games.

What are you waiting for? It's time to train that brain!

Take a close look at this pentagon. How many **TRIANGLES** can you find in it? There are more than you might think! (Answer on page 155)

Write your answer here:

. . . .

When you start looking at things from a new angle, you'll be surprised by what you might find.

Take a minute or two to try and remember these words:

SCARECROW, GLOVES, GREEN, BOX, SKATEBOARD, PIG, SUPERMARKET, BIRTHDAY, HAT.

Cover the words. How many can you remember?

Now your imagination is going to help you remember the words. You just need to create a crazy **CARTOON.**

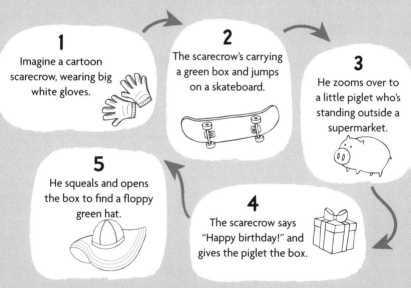

1
Imagine a cartoon scarecrow, wearing big white gloves.

2
The scarecrow's carrying a green box and jumps on a skateboard.

3
He zooms over to a little piglet who's standing outside a supermarket.

4
The scarecrow says "Happy birthday!" and gives the piglet the box.

5
He squeals and opens the box to find a floppy green hat.

Read the story three times, and picture the cartoon in your head. Then try remembering the words again. Thanks to the cartoon, you're more likely to remember them!

SUDOKU puzzles help focus your mind and get you thinking creatively as you try to find solutions.

Fill all the empty squares so every row, column, and 2x2 box contains a circle, square, heart, and star. (Answer on page 155.)

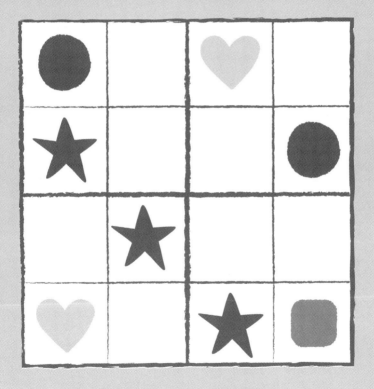

Turn the page to tackle an even trickier Sudoku.

Can you complete this number Sudoku? Fill all the empty squares so every row, column, and 3x3 box contains the numbers 1 to 9. (Answer on page 156.)

	5	6		4	8	2		
2	4	3		7				5
			3	2		6		7
3			7			4		8
		5		9				2
8	7	1		5	4	3		
5					2		6	1
6	3	2		1			8	
9		4	5	8		7		

Now what if we replace numbers with letters? Place a letter from A to I into each empty square so that every row, column. and bold-lined shape contains each letter once. (Answer on page 156.)

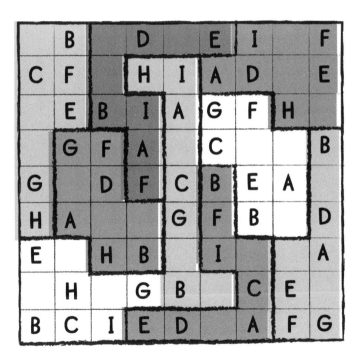

FOLLOW YOUR FEELINGS.

If it feels right, move forward. If it doesn't feel right, don't do it.

OPRAH WINFREY

ACTRESS, TELEVISION HOST, AND PHILANTHROPIST

Can you complete these **MAZES** and spot which two are identical? (Answers on page 156.)

A

B

C

D

E

F

Is your brain starting to feel fired up? Now, try solving these **RIDDLES!**
(Answers on page 156.)

1
What kind of tree can you carry in your hand?

2
Which word is written incorrectly in a dictionary?

3
What is so delicate that saying its name breaks it?

4
What can be seen once in a minute, twice in a moment, but never in a hundred years?

5
What word becomes shorter when you add two letters to it?

Turn on the TV and watch a show as you spend three minutes trying to **MEMOR!ZE** these things.

Now cover the top of this page and list the objects pictured.

....

....

....

How did you do? Try this exercise again, but this time turn the TV off when you try to memorize the things.

....

....

....

Did you do better the second time? Most of us find it easier to remember things when we're not distracted!

I think anyone can do **ANYTHING** they dream of if they put their **MIND** to it, and put in the work.

SHAWN MENDES

SINGER AND SONGWRITER

Can you complete these **NUMBER PYRAMIDS**? The value of
each square is the sum of the two squares directly beneath it.
(Answers on page 157.)

PUZZLE 1

284

120 122

61

34

15 17 10 24

TOP TIP!
Start with the easier
sums at the bottom
of the pyramid and
work your way up!

PUZZLE 2

245

123 113

64 59

25 31 28

13 20 17 9

A **MNEMONIC** (say nuh-monic) is a clever **MEMORY TRICK** that helps you remember things. Check out these examples:

This mnemonic helps us learn the points on a compass, North, South, East, and West.

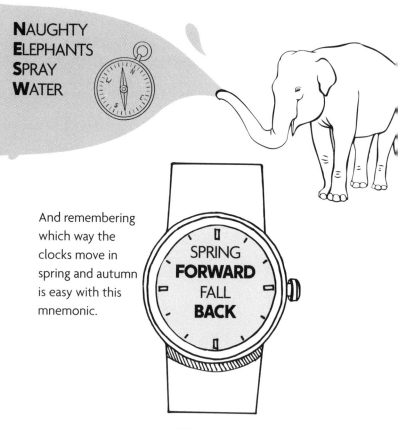

NAUGHTY
ELEPHANTS
SPRAY
WATER

And remembering which way the clocks move in spring and autumn is easy with this mnemonic.

SPRING
FORWARD
FALL
BACK

Mnemonics are also great for remembering how to spell tricky words. Can you figure out which words these mnemonics help spell?

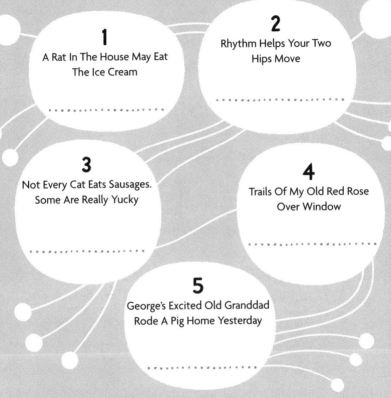

1

A Rat In The House May Eat The Ice Cream

2

Rhythm Helps Your Two Hips Move

3

Not Every Cat Eats Sausages. Some Are Really Yucky

4

Trails Of My Old Red Rose Over Window

5

George's Excited Old Granddad Rode A Pig Home Yesterday

Now try to create your own mnemonic.
What do you need help remembering? It could be anything: players on your favorite football team, capital cities, or something else entirely!

There are other ways to remember tricky things too. One great tip is to try using your **SENSES**. Just think of what you want to remember and then imagine it smells or tastes like something random!

For example, let's say you don't want to forget a number. Imagining it tastes like peanut butter will help you remember it.

1
Picture the number you're trying to remember. Imagine it in 3-D and make it really stand out in your mind with a bright color.

3
Remember the taste of peanut butter, and what it feels like in your mouth. How do you feel when you eat it?

2
Now think of peanut butter. What does it look and smell like?

4
Now picture the number and take a big bite out of it. Imagine that it tastes of peanut butter!

It sounds bonkers but making this kind of connection really helps when you're trying to remember something.

Sit quietly for three minutes and try to remember the **WORDS** below. Then turn the page...

mouse DOG

KANGAROO *glasses*

BLANKET **IGLOO**

TIGER *flower*

BOOK GUITAR

DOOR TOMATO

BOWL GORiLLA

apple TRUCK

WATER BIKE

Which words are missing? Looking at the previous page isn't allowed.

. . . . **DOG**

KANGAROO *glasses*

. . . . **IGLOO**

. . . . *flower*

BOOK . . . .

DOOR . . . .

BOWL . . . .

apple TRUCK

. . . . BIKE

How many words did you remember? Now try this exercise again, but this time when you're memorizing the words, picture each set in your head, and make the image as **STRANGE** as possible. For instance, you could visualize a dog dancing about with a little mouse singing on his head!

Did you remember more words the second time round?

Letter **CLUES** are a great way to remember information. Take this quick test and if you're not sure of the answer, use the letter after each question to help you remember. (Answers on page 157.)

1
What is a female goat called?
N

2
What fairy-tale character has really long hair?
R

3
What is a group of dogs known as?
P

4
Which country features a maple leaf on its flag?
C

5
Name Japan's traditional wrestling sport!
S

6
What is a baby whale called?
C

7
Which planet did Superman come from?
K

8
What is the world's largest land animal?
E

How did the clues help with your answers? Next time you're trying to remember a name, run through the alphabet, and it should jog your memory when you reach the right letter.

FIND YOUR INNER UNICORN!

In one day we can feel all sorts of things—happy, sad, annoyed, angry, excited, hungry (in fact I'm always feeling hungry). But no matter how you're feeling, it's good to be aware of your emotions. Feelings help us understand the world around us and enjoy ourselves.

For instance, if you notice a situation gets on your nerves, you can avoid doing it again in the future. Or if something turns out to be really good fun, you can aim to do it more!

Being aware of feelings also helps us get along with people better. How someone is feeling affects the way we communicate with them. If they're really excited, their mood will rub off on you and make you feel enthusiastic too. Or if you're talking to a friend who's feeling a bit sad, you'll probably want to try and cheer them up.

Our phones and tablets give us lots of ways to communicate and connect with people via methods ranging from emails and direct messages to social media posts, texts, and more.

But even with all these different ways to stay in touch, it seems technology can often actually break our confidence and leave us feeling disconnected from the world. So when you next feel down or sad, turn to this chapter and boost your happiness. It's full of ways to help you feel good, get in touch with your emotions, and shine like the star you are.

Ready?

Let's find your inner unicorn!

Unicorns are beautiful, magical creatures. Fill this one with all the things that make you **SPECIAL**.

IF YOU GET STUCK,
ASK A **FRIEND** WHAT
THEY THINK MAKES YOU
SPECIAL!

What **NEGATIVE** thoughts have you had recently? Fill these thought bubbles with them.

ONCE YOU'RE DONE, **SCRIBBLE** OVER THE THOUGHTS TO **BANISH** THEM!

Now fill the thought bubbles on this page with POSITIVE
things you've thought about.

GIVE THESE POSITIVE
THOUGHTS SOME
HAPPY COLORS
ONCE YOU'RE DONE!

It's natural to think negatively sometimes, but looking on the bright side
boosts our emotions. If you notice yourself feeling negative, remind yourself
of all the things in life you feel grateful for.

Can you find the correct words to complete these **EMPOWERING** quotes? Choose your answers from the box on the opposite page if you need help. Be warned: there are extra words in there to make it harder! (Answers on page 157.)

1

"Your self-worth is determined by .... You don't have to depend on .... telling you who you are."
BEYONCÉ

2

"Be yourself, be happy, be ...., be strong and just have fun."
JOJO SIWA

3

"All our dreams can come true— if we have the .... to pursue them!"
WALT DISNEY

HURRY FOOTBALL SWEETS
DISTANT COURAGE CONFIDENT
orange NEARBY PIGLET umbrella
SOMEONE pretend SURPRISE
DONKEY TEACUP YOU SILLY
FUNNY knees balloons

Now think up some empowering sayings of your own.
Write them here:

If you get stuck, think about people or situations that you
find inspiring!

89

Life is too **SHORT**
to surround yourself
with people who don't

make you **HAPPY**.
Follow your own track!

LUCY HALE

ACTRESS AND SINGER

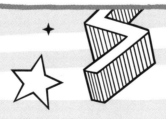

Get in touch with your inner unicorn and **GLOW FOR IT** with this golden visualization exercise.

2. Imagine the golden light sparkling with magical, positive energy as it grows bigger.

3. Feel your inner power growing stronger, as the golden light fills you with confidence and happiness.

1. Close your eyes and take a deep breath. Now picture a sparkly golden light glowing around you!

4. Tap into these feelings throughout the day by imagining the golden light glowing all around you!

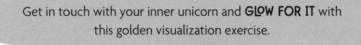

Keeping a **JOURNAL** is a great way to help you feel happy and get more creative. Follow these tips, and you'll be journaling in no time.

WRITE ON!

Try to write in your journal, every day if you can. Fill it with whatever you want, such as happy thoughts or positive moments.

MAKE IT SPECIAL

Express yourself in your journal. Use stickers, colored pens, drawings, and anything else you want! You might even want to stick in photos, tickets, or special mementos too.

FUN ZONE

Journaling doesn't have to be perfect. Don't worry if there's a spelling mistake or if a page looks messy—that's all part of the fun!

Use this page as a trial run for your journal.

Now just decide what you're going to write and you're ready to go!

Being **KIND** to people doesn't just cheer them up, it makes our body produce a special chemical that increases our self-esteem and makes us feel optimistic.

Use this page to record the ways you've been kind in the past or could show kindness in the future.

Circle any of the words on this page that you find **INSPIRING**.

LAUGH adventure AWARE

Sing BELIEVE CONFIDENT

Free

AMAZING courage FUN

CHALLENGE

UNICORN

SURPRISE LOVE Open

HELPFUL Special MUSIC

ENERGY SUCCESS Colorful

CARING Happy ENJOY

Miracle

Wonderful

Brilliant THANKFUL

SMILE

Sparkle CALM

CREATIVE DREAM LEARN

Feeling inspired boosts our enthusiasm and focus!

You don't need
DIRECTIONS.
Just point yourself to
the **TOP** and **GO**.

**DWAYNE "THE ROCK"
JOHNSON**
ACTOR, PRODUCER, AND FORMER WRESTLER

List at least ten of your friend's **BEST** qualities in this box. Then doodle a picture of them.

Once you're done, turn the page and hand the book to your friend.

Use this box to list at least ten things you 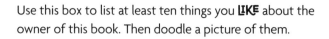 about the owner of this book. Then doodle a picture of them.

Compare this page and the last one to see what qualities you have in common. The more personal stuff we share with our friends, the stronger our friendships become!

Getting outdoors with your family is a great way to make fun **MEMORIES** and embark on new **ADVENTURES**. Give these suggestions a try and then add more things you'd like to do.

☆ Go on a bug safari at your local park

☆ Make a feast or picnic and eat it outside

☆ Organize a scavenger hunt

☆ Take a four-legged friend for a walk

☆ Have a wild woodland bicycle ride

☆ Make a nature collage

☆ ....

☆ ....

☆ ....

☆ ....

☆ ....

☆ ....

☆ ....

Positive **AFFIRMATIONS** are phrases that help you think happy thoughts and make you feel good. Check out these examples:

I'm proud to
be me and
feel really
CONFIDENT!

I deserve to
be **HAPPY!**

I am full of
POSITIVITY
and kindness!

I'm a **GOOD**
person. I am
beautiful inside
and out!

Affirmations work best
when they're repeated
every day. Find
somewhere private
and try saying each
of these affirmations
twenty times, out loud.

Use these tips to create your own positive affirmations.

1
Make each affirmation short so it's easier to remember.

2
You're repeating the affirmations to help you, so be sure to start them with "I" or "My."

3
Write your affirmations in the present tense. For instance, "I am happy" rather than "I will be happy."

Try writing some affirmations here.

We don't need to rely on technology to find out about the people in our lives. Use these questions to **INTERVIEW** a friend or family member and see what you learn about them.

QUESTIONS

Which actor would you like to meet and why?

If you were an animal, what would you be and why?

What makes you laugh?

What's your superpower?

What's the best thing about being you and why?

Describe your favorite place in the world.

Now get your friend or family member to interview you!

Asking questions is a great way to get a conversation going and learn surprising new things about people. Write some more questions to ask here.

Think about these questions:
What did you discover about your friend?
How does this make you feel about them?
Who do you want to interview next and why?

Sometimes in **LIFE** you don't always feel like a **WINNER** but that doesn't mean you're not a **WINNER**.

LADY GAGA

SINGER, SONGWRITER, AND ACTRESS

Check off all the **FEELINGS** below that you've felt.

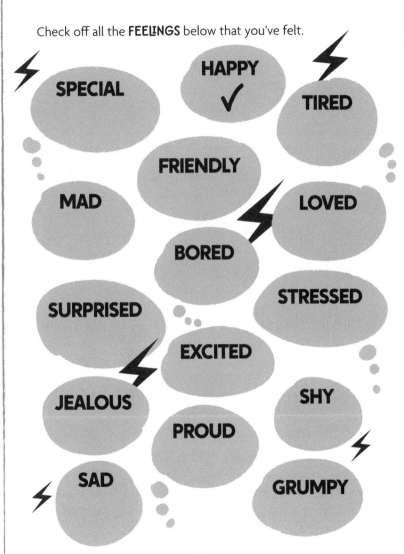

SPECIAL

HAPPY ✓

TIRED

FRIENDLY

MAD

LOVED

BORED

STRESSED

SURPRISED

EXCITED

JEALOUS

SHY

PROUD

SAD

GRUMPY

Now ask a friend to check off all of the **FEELINGS** they've felt.

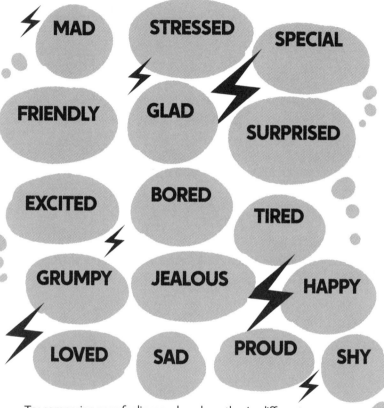

MAD

STRESSED

SPECIAL

FRIENDLY

GLAD

SURPRISED

EXCITED

BORED

TIRED

GRUMPY

JEALOUS

HAPPY

LOVED

SAD

PROUD

SHY

Try comparing your feelings and see how they're different.

There are no right or wrong answers when it comes to feelings. All of your emotions combine to make you the wonderful, sensitive person you are!

Add your
fingerprints to
this page. They
are completely
INDIVIDUAL,
just like you.

IN A WORLD OF
7.7 BILLION
PEOPLE, YOU ARE
ONE OF A **KIND**.

TIME OUT!

Picture yourself kicking back at the end of the day. Where are you and what are you doing? Maybe you're imagining yourself getting sleepy in front of the TV? Or perhaps you're picturing yourself snuggled up and nodding off in bed?

Getting enough rest keeps us healthy, helps us concentrate, and has a positive effect on our memory. It also affects our mood and how we understand and deal with things. So it's really important that we relax properly and get enough sleep. It's what recharges our batteries!

Now think about relaxing again. Do you have your phone with you? Is it in your pocket or are you holding it? Maybe you're even using it to relax?

While it can be a fun distraction, the technology in our lives is designed to be stimulating, which is the opposite of winding down. In fact, research has shown that overusing phones can disturb our sleep and leave us feeling stressed.

It's no wonder really. Phone screens emit a blue light, which stops our body from releasing melatonin, a chemical that makes us sleepy. And with notifications popping up, messages and emails to reply to, social media posts to catch up on, addictive games to play, TV shows and films to watch, plus other apps to use and the whole of the internet to look at, if you use your phone a lot, it can easily get a bit much.

This chapter is all about relaxing, finding your inner power, and enjoying each moment. Complete the exercises on the following pages, and they will have you feeling calm and confident in no time.

Would you like to *really* relax?

Take a deep breath and read on...

There are so many ways to kick back and take a break from technology. How do you like to relax?

Circle the stuff you've done or would like to do, then add more ideas to this **BUCKET LIST.**

READ A BOOK

CATCH UP WITH FRIENDS

RIDE A BIKE

Play football

GET DANCING

Go to the movies

Paint a portrait

Go dog walking

VISIT A MUSEUM

BAKE COOKIES

HAVE A WATER BALLOON BATTLE

Play board games

MAKE AMAZING SLIME

Never stop adding things to your bucket list. They are a great reminder of all the fun stuff life has to offer!

Allow yourself to be in the

MOMENT,

and appreciate the moment.

HAPPINESS will follow.

RICHARD BRANSON

BUSINESSMAN, AUTHOR, AND PHILANTHROPIST

Do your shoulders feel tense or achy sometimes? Using a smartphone or tablet can have an effect on our posture. Try this easy stretch to **BANISH** any aches or tension.

Stand with your arms by your side and your feet hip-distance apart.

Breathe in and gently lift your shoulders up toward your ears.

1,2,3

Hold your shoulders up like this for the count of three. Then gently lower them as you breathe out.

Repeat this five times, and your shoulders will soon start to feel loose and more relaxed. Phew!

Noticing things **AS THEY HAPPEN** helps you **ENJOY** them more. Try this easy exercise to help you tap into the here and now!

IF YOUR MIND **DRIFTS** OFF, JUST GENTLY COME **BACK** TO THE EXERCISE.

4

Next, focus on your left leg and feel it relax. Do the same with your right leg.

5

Move upward and focus on the different parts of your body, feeling them relax one by one.

6

When your whole body is feeling more relaxed, open your eyes and stretch.

Try practicing this exercise every day; it'll get EASIER each time you do it!

You can't really go **WRONG** as long as you're **TRUE TO YOURSELF**.

BLAKE LIVELY

ACTRESS

Concentrating and focusing on doing something intently with your hands is another great way to relax. Get creative and **COLOR** this wavy, curvy pattern.

Coloring lets you enjoy the moment as well as use your creative flair.

Want to tap into your **INNER POWER**? This fun visualization and meditation will help.

Get comfortable, close your eyes, and take a few deep breaths.

Imagine you're in a peaceful forest. What does it look like?

What does the animal look like? What is their name?

Now picture a beautiful, friendly animal joining you.

Imagine feeling calm and confident with the animal by your side.

Then, when you're ready, open your eyes!

This creature is now your animal guide. Want to feel more confident or calm? Just close your eyes and picture your animal guide!

Draw or write about your **ANIMAL GUIDE** on this page.

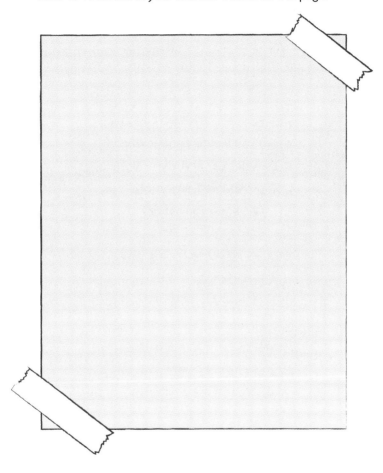

Use as much detail as possible to strengthen your bond.

Imagine your emotions are like the colors of a **RAINBOW.** Orange might be your favorite color, but the other colors are just as important. And our feelings are just the same. Happiness might be our favorite feeling, but we need all of our emotions, even the ones that don't make us feel great.

Sit down somewhere quiet and close your eyes. What colors are you feeling right now? Do you feel a happy yellow glow inside? Or maybe you feel a grumpy purple glow? Perhaps there's a red, angry color somewhere? What do you notice?

Whatever you're feeling, accept that's how things are at the moment. You don't need to change anything or do anything differently. Just feel the way you feel and accept that's how it is right now. Emotions come and go, just like rainbows. This is how you feel now, but it's not forever. Moods change, and you'll probably feel like a different color later.

Tune in to your emotions rainbow whenever you can. Staying in touch with how you're feeling will help you understand how things affect you.

Now draw your **EMOTIONS RAINBOW** and make the colors you're feeling right now bigger and bolder!

Come back to this page at the end of the day and see how the colors you're feeling have changed.

Mandalas are cool designs that contain geometric patterns. They've been used for thousands of years in the Buddhist and Hindu traditions as spiritual and ritual symbols. **COLOR** these mandalas. Once you're finished, try drawing your own.

123

This yummy exercise will help you **ENJOY** each moment ...

YOU WILL NEED
* A bar of chocolate
* Somewhere quiet
* A cushion or comfy chair
* Did I mention chocolate?

Get comfortable somewhere you won't be disturbed.

Look at the chocolate as you hold it.

How heavy is it? What does the chocolate feel like?

What color is it? What does it smell like?

Notice your mouth. Is it watering?! OK, go ahead and take a bite.

What does the chocolate feel like as it melts? How does it taste?

Is this the longest you've ever had a piece of chocolate in your mouth?!

Go on, then. You'd better eat it!

THIS **EXERCISE** IS FUN TO TRY WITH A **FRIEND!**

Draw a picture of the moment you ate the chocolate.

Draw the weirdest thing you've ever eaten.

Now draw the yummiest thing you've ever scarfed.

Paying attention when you eat makes food seem tastier and more enjoyable. It also helps us notice when we're full.

A dream board is a collection of inspirational goodies displayed on a cork board. They're a great way to highlight things that make you **HAPPY.**

What will you put on your dream board? Add more stuff to this list to start you off.

song words
PET PiCTURES
Doodles
PICTURES

QUOTES
WISH LIST
PHOTOS

TOP TIPS

1
Don't worry about making your dream board perfect. You can change things as you go along.

2
Put your dream board somewhere you'll see it every day!

3
Update your dream board whenever it feels right.

Collect quotes and song lyrics for your dream board here.

Making a dream board is a fun way to focus on the future and your happiness!

BREATHE
IN
BREATHE
OUT

Do you ever reach for your phone if you're having trouble getting to **SLEEP**?

Next time, try doing **THIS** instead of turning to technology...

Lie in bed with your arms relaxed by your sides and get comfortable.

Slowly breathe in through your nose to the count of four.

Hold your breath for a couple of seconds.

Exhale through your mouth for the count of four and say the word "relax" in your mind.

Repeat these steps and feel your body become calmer as your mind lets go, leaving you ready to fall into a peaceful, deep sleep.

Focusing on your breathing relaxes the muscles in your body and helps you feel calm.

BE
BRUTAL!

What are you usually like in the morning? Do you leap out of bed, ready for a day full of fun and adventures? Or do you slowly emerge, half asleep, and take a while to properly wake up?

We're all different and we all wake up differently. But we all do similar stuff each morning: eat breakfast, wash our face, brush our teeth, get dressed, and so on. Our brains recognize that we repeat certain stuff and make it into a habit. Which explains how you sometimes do things on autopilot, like leaving the house fully dressed, even though you don't really remember putting your clothes on.

Our brains do this because habits use less energy. We don't need to relearn how to put on a T-shirt every time we get dressed, or figure out how to eat a piece of toast during breakfast, so our brain saves energy and makes the actions into a habit. Clever, eh?

However, there are good habits and there are bad ones! Good habits include things like remembering to exercise and finishing work. Bad habits can include having too many treats and doing work at the last minute! Everyone has good and bad habits, but what's important is to try and be aware of the things you do automatically, so you can watch out for stuff that wastes your time or makes you feel bad.

For instance, there's nothing wrong with zoning out on our phone sometimes. But it can become a problem when you're so used to zoning out that it becomes a habit, and you end up doing it all the time—even when you're hanging out with friends!

This chapter will help you enjoy the good parts of technology and avoid the bad bits. It's packed with easy exercises and fun ways to take more control of your tech, from tackling phubbing (see pages 134–135) and finding cool apps, to saying "no" to notifications, choosing who to follow and unfollow, and much more.

Ready to be brutal?

Let's get to it!

Fill this side with things you **LOVE** about your phone.

Fill this side with things you **DON'T LOVE** about it.

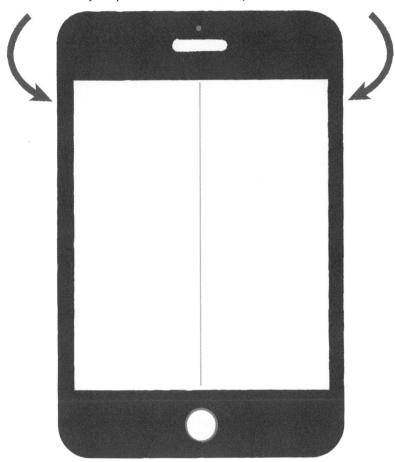

It's good to find out which parts of being on your phone you enjoy and which bits are bad news, so you can concentrate on using it to get the positive stuff!

Phubbing, or "phone snubbing," means snubbing someone by looking at your phone instead of paying attention to them.

Which of these descriptions describe phubbing? Check off your answers.

Keeping your phone in sight when you're chatting with a friend.

Having your phone on the table at meal times.

Checking your phone if a conversation dries up.

#P

Looking at your phone when someone's talking to you.

Answering a call when you're in the middle of talking to someone.

Texting or calling someone while you're at a party.

How many phrases did you check? Would you be surprised to hear that they **ALL** describe phubbing?

AVOID **PHUBBING** BY TURNING ON AIRPLANE MODE WHEN YOU'RE **WITH** OTHER **PEOPLE!**

Phubbing can be seen as **RUDE** and **ANTISOCIAL**. Take this quiz and answer **A**, **B**, or **C** to find out how phubbing affects you.

1. You can't think what to say to your friend. Do you...
A) Message someone else
B) Show them a video on your phone
C) Ask them a question

2. You get a text when you're chatting with a friend in person. Do you...
A) Read the text
B) Check the text once you're finished
C) Ignore it—a text can wait until later

3. Your friend video chats you as you're eating dinner. Do you...
A) Pick up and ignore whoever you're with
B) Answer but tell your friend you'll call them back
C) Leave it and get back to them after the meal

MOSTLY A – Phubbing alert! Sorry, but some people may be upset by the way you use your phone.

MOSTLY B—Epic! You watch out for phubbing and manage to avoid doing it, most of the time.

MOSTLY C—Yay! You always try to put people first and are a phubbing-free zone. Cool!

Want to avoid scrolling through endless posts? Use this checklist to work out who to **FOLLOW** and **UNFOLLOW**!

How does looking at the person's feed make you feel?

FRUSTRATED   **BORED**

HAPPY   **INSPIRED**

IMPRESSED   **JEALOUS**

How would you describe their posts?

PERFECT   **INTERESTING**

DULL   **FUNNY**

SMUG   **MEAN**

How often do they post?

HARDLY EVER   **2 OR 3 TIMES A WEEK**

ONCE A MONTH   **2 OR 3 TIMES A DAY**

ONCE A WEEK   **TOO MUCH!**

Carefully choose whom you follow, and if someone you follow is mean or makes you feel bad, ask yourself if they still deserve your time and attention.

Whenever you pick up your phone, ask yourself if you really want to use it or whether you're picking it up out of habit.

Take a **PICTURE** of this page and use it as your lock-screen wallpaper. That way you'll remember to check each time you're tempted to pick up your phone!

Check off the things you look for in an app!

EXCITING

CUTE

CALMING

STIMULATING

inspirational

POPULAR

USEFUL

SOCIAL

EDUCATIONAL

FUN

ADDICTIVE

COOL

HANDY

UPLIFTING

TRENDING

EMPOWERING

Next time you download an app, try using this checklist to help you pick something you'll **REALLY LIKE.**

TOP TIPS FOR AWESOME APPS

SPRING CLEAN!
Got any apps you haven't used for a while? **DELETE** them and free up space on your device. You can always download them again if you want to.

GAME OVER
Watch out for apps that waste your time. If they draw you in and trick you into using them for hours with no real payoff, maybe it's time to get rid of them?

FEEL-GOOD FACTOR
Whenever you download an app, ask yourself what you'll be getting out of using it. Only go for useful apps or ones that make you feel good!

139

Over the next day, keep track of when and why you use your phone or tablet, and how using it makes you **FEEL**.

MORNING

AFTERNOON

EVENING

Count how many times your phone distracts you through the day!

Think about these questions at the end of the day:
What did you notice about using your phone?
What surprises you about how you use it?
How do you feel about this information?

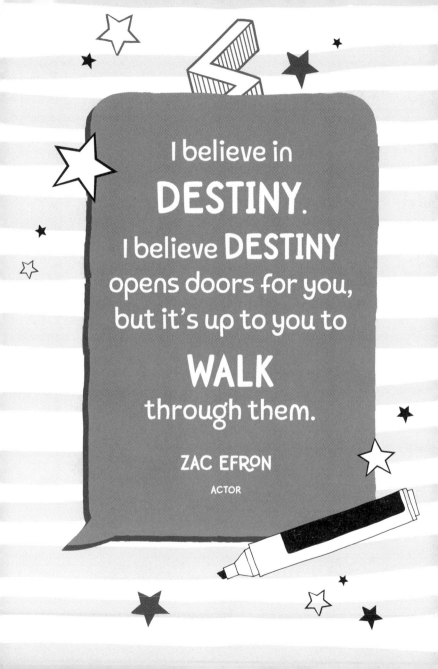

I believe in **DESTINY**. I believe **DESTINY** opens doors for you, but it's up to you to **WALK** through them.

ZAC EFRON

ACTOR

Find the famous apps hidden in this grid and cross them out!
(Answers on page 157.)

INSTAGRAM **TWITTER** **YOUTUBE**
SNAPCHAT **TIKTOK** **FACEBOOK**

Z	N	E	R	G	H	T	S	A	I
Y	W	S	U	P	L	I	D	P	N
O	O	S	U	H	Z	K	O	O	S
U	V	N	I	F	G	T	N	B	T
T	C	A	E	L	I	O	S	K	A
U	F	P	L	T	H	K	H	O	G
B	S	C	T	W	I	T	T	E	R
E	U	H	A	D	C	W	I	Z	A
Y	F	A	C	E	B	O	O	K	M
X	Q	T	I	Q	W	T	A	S	T

Now try **DELETING** one of your social media apps for real! You can still check your account through a browser. But deleting the app will make your account slightly harder to use, giving you more control over when you use it.

DELETE the app and check this box once you're done!

Have you ever noticed how **DISTRACTING** notifications can be? Each time one pops up on your phone, it's the same as someone tapping you on your shoulder, pestering you to look at your phone—again and again and *again*!

What would you say to someone who kept doing that? Write it here:

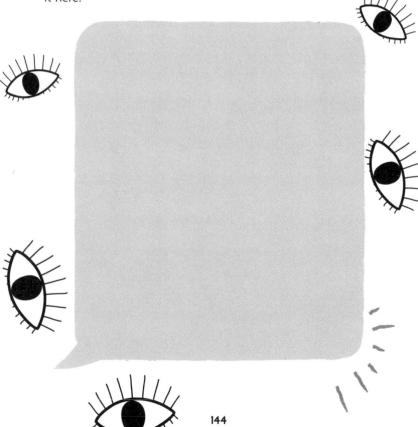

An easy way to stop this kind of thing happening is to **TURN OFF** your social media notifications. So, head to your settings and turn them off, **NOW.**

TAKE **CONTROL** AND TURN OFF YOUR **NOTIFICATIONS!**

Off

You don't have to keep them off forever, but it's a good way to figure out which notifications you don't need to have distracting you throughout your day.

We have to remember to give **OURSELVES** a bit of a PAT ON THE BACK and say, "You've done really **WELL** today."

FEARNE COTTON

ENGLISH PRESENTER AND AUTHOR

A lot of people charge their phone in the bedroom. However, this makes it much easier to use your phone when it's time to **WIND DOWN**.

Where do you **CURRENTLY** charge your phone?

LIST other places you can charge your phone.

If you charge your device in your bedroom, try charging it somewhere new, especially when you go to sleep. This will stop you from being distracted at night and hopefully help you sleep better too.

Think you could spend an **ENTIRE** day without the internet? Try it and then draw a picture of what your internet-free day looked like.

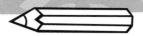

Write about it in this box.

What was **DIFFERENT**?

What did you **ENJOY** most?

How did your day without the internet **FEEL**?

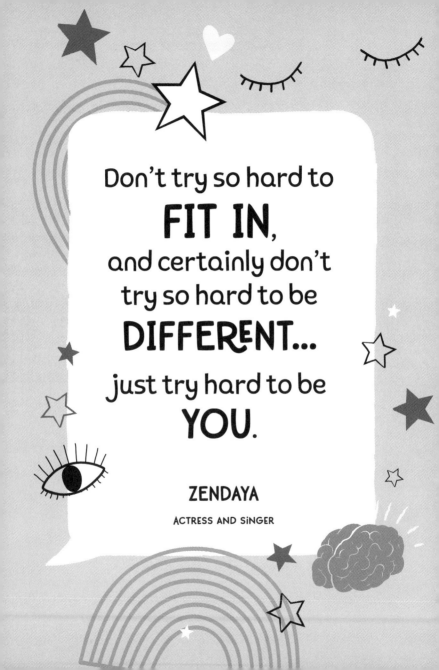

Don't try so hard to **FIT IN,** and certainly don't try so hard to be **DIFFERENT...** just try hard to be **YOU.**

ZENDAYA

ACTRESS AND SINGER

Hey! You've reached the end of this book! I hope it's helped you feel more creative and given you more time to do new things. Draw or write about how you feel here.

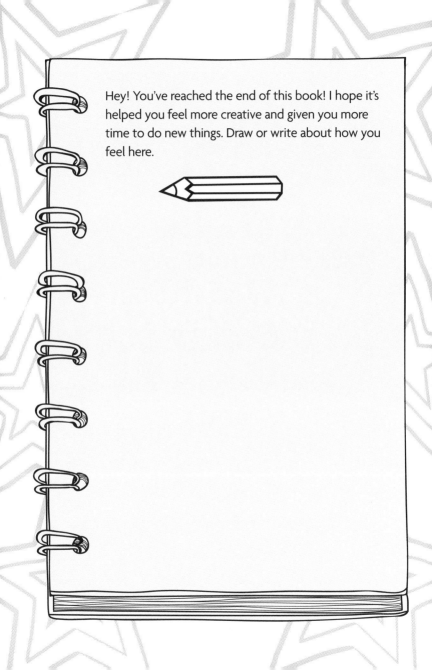

CONCLUSION

Congratulations for completing **BRAVER STRONGER SMARTER!** I hope you've found the exercises in this book enjoyable and enlightening, and they've helped you take a break from the hustle and bustle of online life. But if you find technology starts to take over again, be sure to revisit your favorite pages to help you get back on top of things.

Keep working at tuning in to the here and now too. Don't worry if it takes a while to get the hang of it. Keep practicing and you'll be an expert in no time.

This book is really only the beginning of your journey. All any of us can do is try our best. Some days things will go well and other days might be less successful. But as long as you're trying and keeping an eye on things, you'll be heading in the right direction!

I hope you continue to enjoy the technology in your life and use it to serve you well!

Love,
VINCENT

PUZZLE ANSWERS

65

There are 10 triangles here.

There are 5 of these triangles.

There are 5 of these triangles.

There are 5 of these triangles.

There are 10 of these triangles.

SO THERE ARE 35 TRiANGLES iN TOTAL!

67

68

7	5	6	1	4	8	2	3	9
2	4	3	6	7	9	8	1	5
1	9	8	3	2	5	6	4	7
3	2	9	7	6	1	4	5	8
4	6	5	8	9	3	1	7	2
8	7	1	2	5	4	3	9	6
5	8	7	4	3	2	9	6	1
6	3	2	9	1	7	5	8	4
9	1	4	5	8	6	7	2	3

69

A	B	C	D	H	E	I	G	F
C	F	G	H	I	A	D	B	E
D	E	B	I	A	G	F	H	C
I	G	F	A	E	C	H	D	B
G	I	D	F	C	B	E	A	H
H	A	E	C	G	F	B	I	D
E	D	H	B	F	I	G	C	A
F	H	A	G	B	D	C	E	I
B	C	I	E	D	H	A	F	G

71

Mazes a and f are identical.

A F

B

C

D

E

72

1 A palm, **2** Incorrectly, **3** Silence, **4** The letter *m*, **5** Short.

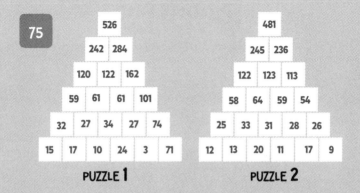

75

PUZZLE 1

		526			
	242	284			
	120	122	162		
	59	61	61	101	
32	27	34	27	74	
15	17	10	24	3	71

PUZZLE 2

		481			
	245	236			
	122	123	113		
	58	64	59	54	
25	33	31	28	26	
12	13	20	11	17	9

81

1 Nanny, 2 Rapunzel, 3 Pack, 4 Canada, 5 Sumo, 6 Calf, 7 Krypton, 8 Elephant.

88

1 You, Someone, 2 Confident, 3 Courage.

143

```
Z N E R G H T S A I
Y W S U P L I D P N
O O S U H Z K O O S
U V N I F G T N B T
T C A E L I O S K A
U F P L T H K H O G
B S C T W I T T E R
E U H A D C W I T A
Y F A C E B O O K M
X Q T I Q W T A S T
```

157

QUOTES
In order of appearance

"Miley Cyrus Plays With Puppies (While Answering Fan Questions)." YouTube, October 11, 2017. https://www.youtube.com/watch?v=TRviREiY1jg.

Corcoran, Monica. "Katy Perry Kisses and Tells." *Women's Health*, March 9, 2009. https://www.womenshealthmag.com/food/a19925692/katy-perry-interview.

Schriffen, John, Nick Poppy and Dave Kovenetsky. "Venus Williams Courts Success in Fashion, Fun...and Tennis." Yahoo! News, April 25, 2013. https://www.yahoo.com/news/blogs/newsmakers/venus-williams-courts-success-fashion-fun-tennis-023044860.html.

Thompson, Krissah. "The nine important things Michelle Obama and Oprah said last night." *Washington Post*, June 15, 2016. https://www.washingtonpost.com/news/arts-and-entertainment/wp/2016/06/15/the-nine-important-things-michelle-obama-and-oprah-said-last-night/.

Xue, Faith. "Ariana Grande Shares her #1 Beauty Tip (and it's not what you'd expect." Byrdie, September 2, 2016. https://www.byrdie.co.uk/ariana-grande-beauty-tips.

Helbig, Grace. *Grace's Guide: The Art of Pretending to Be Grown-Up*. New York: Touchstone, Simon & Schuster, 2014.

Cooke, Rachel. "Big Briton." *The Guardian*, November 11, 2007. https://www.theguardian.com/stage/2007/nov/11/television.comedy.

"Text of J. K. Rowling's Speech." *Harvard Gazette*, June 5, 2008. https://news.harvard.edu/gazette/story/2008/06/text-of-j-k-rowling-speech/.

"Ellen DeGeneres at Tulane's 2009 Commencement Speech." YouTube, May 18, 2009. https://www.youtube.com/watch?v=0e8ToRVOtRo.

"Oprah talks to graduates about feelings, failure and finding happiness." *Stanford News*, June 15, 2008. https://news.stanford.edu/news/2008/june18/como-061808.html.

Johnson Jr., Billy. "Shawn Mendes Talks About Inspiring Fans, Being Inspired by John Mayer." Yahoo! News, March 20, 2017. https://uk.news.yahoo.com/shawn-mendes-talks-about-inspiring-fans-and-being-inspired-by-john-mayer-214619096.html.